Red

Shwetanjali

Made with ❤ on the BookLeaf Publishing Platform
www.bookleafpub.in
www.bookleafpub.com

Dedication

Red has been my favourite colour ever since, and I know,
Bu, you've *always* remembered it.

I dedicate this book to all the readers who have always
longed too hard all in the hopes for that one last time;
I get you.

Preface

To be honest, longing is the sickest feeling of all.

Acknowledgements

This book will always be a dream come true. I could never imagine writing these poems without the countless moments I've felt hurt, lost, or simply too much out of life. There will always be parts of us we desperately wish to silence or let go of, but since life is such a vast roller coaster — a puzzle with no perfect pieces — I'm afraid that goodbyes will always remain coy.

Still, I'll always be grateful for both the nightmares and the daydreams this living offers; like roses with thorns, they complete the beauty of existence. And it's okay, believe me — it'll always be okay.

To all the faces and memories that inspired these poems, thank you.
Living itself is the reason reality feels like such an irony.

Hope you enjoy.
Happy creepy reading!

1. Hollow

I feel sorry sometimes that I love you to the full
Whatever my heart can bear, I give it all to you
Scratching the corners, the exsectra left in the shadows
My heart feels sorry that I love you to hollow.

I had a piece of paper, a thing to write to you
My fingers hovering below my chin, my endless mood
I peak a glance at your sight, at your beautiful silhouette
And see all the stars and moon clustered into you

Today was important, today you came too
I wonder how many times I have counted your absence
in the room
Your breath just sweet and sober, coming to me
Your voice like desserts singing, like rivers flowing
beneath

Your voice reaches me first, your sight the second
I love you enough to let me know i am not paranoid for
your presence

Your shadows and your smiles and your every little
dance
It's dancing in my mind, moving waves in my heart

I hope to tell you someday, you're more than just my
part
You're the paradise someone's looking for, some already
missed apart
I want to look into your eyes and tell myself
Things I wouldn't want in my heart
Its such a curse to feel you right here.

I stare at you, taking in your beautiful sight
If I looked a bit more, I would choke on this endless
fountain
I want to hear you sing, can you sing for me a bit?
I would like to tell you I'm a singer, a singer for your
rain.

I don't want to forget you, don't want to remember you
like the Haley's comet
If only to ignite my soul, I want to burn in your fire
beneath
You're orange, pink, red and yellow, all the hues mixed in
one
You're just some so serene, so peaceful to my aching
soul.

If only I could corner you to ask if you like me or not,
To put a finger on your chest to warn if it ever beats for
another
There's nothing like this embarrassing shit I know that
you do
You were never the love talk of the town but I wonder if
someone who saw ever loves you.
Still.

I freeze when my mind makes book pairs of characters
And you fit with some another girl who's just too kind to
be seen
But the protagonist's who seeks her and finds her
shining like a diamond under clovers
She's all covered in mud but he pulls her closer
I shiver at the imagination if you'd be with some another
one day
Why can't we grow up now and let me hold you in that
way

Mess it up, its not true even in coming hundred years
I won't ever be yours because I'm walking under ironic
clouds
I'm destroyed and ugly and unkind in the meanest way
You're perfect and beautiful and a gentleman, they
always say.

The catchlights in your eyes when you rarely talk to me
I could stare at them forever and never get bored by the
stream
You're so beautiful it kills me sometimes, like some
figures are dancing in those lights
And taking steps and twisting feet, in a metaphor to tell
you don't belong to me.

And all there's left is this hollow heart inside a rusted
ribcage
A beating heart for a lost love maze
There lies a childish vain, a longing foreseen miles apart
A hollow heart with so much love that its grief after all.

2. Drunk Bee

Its coming true, I'm not even 20 yet
If love was anything but flowers
You would've been my rose
For so long I've longed for something like glass
Something like wind and white feathers
And clean with big letters in white.
So white,
So blinding white.

I'm returning to your throne, I'm walking the steps
This castle could be yours, I could be just a mistress
I could trip on the wine glass and you'll send me to
regret
My choice, my voice, my actions to coming to your
doorstep
To think that you'll heal me when all you'll do would be
to kill and
Kill and kill until there's no version left me
Which has memories of you, your voice and your
melodies

You're so fine, you could touch my heart so well
I'm afraid it will either fly or burn in the heat of this
mystery.

What are you going to say, what is it that you're
planning?
Are you planning to hurt me, are you thinking of dying?
Can you be my lover, it's an abrupt questions isn't it?
Should I ask you while you write or will you do that for
me?

Damn this hunger, this dilemma of your personality
Why are you like this, like a white feather in a coat of
black keys
Take off that slithering cap and show me your true face
Let me see you for who you are, let me know if it's me or
not
Is it or is it not?
Well damn what it is if it isn't me.
Burn what it is if it isn't you and me.

3. Blue cap

I stared into your eyes for long that evening,
Spiders do crawl but their touch can't be felt before your
eyes,
Why are there questions I don't have an answer to inside
my head

You're as pretty as violets blooming in the moonlight
I love your G tone voice and your presence so much.
I know you don't read me though I wish you did
I'm just another wanderer like you

How come we met and I write lines about you
I never cross your mind like I wish I'd do
Maybe once I did, maybe twice across your eyes
The words I desire from your lips still hide

That ac chamber, that throttle event with you
Those singing sessions plus your cap so blue
Sometimes it makes me sick, it grips me to a point
No breath across my lips, just your invisible caress

Let me go on and on today to find the piece within me
The string you pulled, the dreams I see
What is it about you that draws me in, what is it I
believe in about you
I wish you were a closer friend of mine, I wish you were
here

Under the clouds we walk on and on
That salt drink you bought and sipped near me
I smell your scent, I take you in
Without another glance, I read you in me

Your codes locked in my head
My hands itch to touch your hairs
Maybe many eyes on me, but I want yours instead
If your presence was a scent, I'd drown in it

Those lavender clouds that pass by when you're near
I'm scared to look at you with eyes of fear
You won't notice me, you'd pass me by
Such lust for your voice I could hear myself cry

It's literally nothing, this passing feeling
I wish a lot of things upon you and me
That stage play just for you and me
That pink and red and blue flying colours all in my head

They blind my sight, they tell me to run
Either to hide or run into you
I wish you were a haven, a covert hidden from sight
I wish you were not human so that I could be safe and
without a shame

Talk to me, tell me more about you
I wish these things upon you and me
Sing my heart, scream my desperation
There's nothing I've found yet which entice me about
you

You whistle to girls, you don't have much rules
The very thing I desire from myself to bloom
In the night my dreams stroll past your window
I told you I'm just another wanderer finally meeting
someone alike

Maybe I'll go on and on until I find you in me
That space, that breath, any place where you stay
I'll find you and tell you my name
I'll let you remember it for long before we fade

In that rain, my clothes all wet
I entered the café and looked for your eyes
They met, I waved and I saw your eyes rise from me and
falter from the one beside

I waved until you overlooked
Until that magic disappeared, that spark lost its
brightness

But I sat outside, still wet in the rain
I talked of love and stared at you through the pane
You were there, you didn't see me
I wish I was on drugs, hallucinating you with me

But you stepped out the door, damp in your clothes
Then you slowly glanced at my side but I couldn't see
yours
Night with its light ate away our spark
Your eyes walked away and I stared at the dark

Your back, your slick hairs
Your ride back home without my care
You are annoying, you're carless but you like me I know
I'm my favourite person but you can still be some more

Slightly better I'll surpass your surmise someday
I'll become better and I'll forget you just like that
But you were here in my way, someday I'll remember
This fire in me won't let me scramble
I'll rise and you'll forget this spark
You'll play along and I'll share my part.

4. Sword

How meaningless could it be
You on my front porch
In your eyes, no tempt, I see
Soft blue lights may not brighten my sight
But your face is all I remember in the dark.

When you sit with me and tell your sorrow
To fight the king and rescue your morrow
I know life is ruthless, it isn't always forgiving
But what sins did I commit
To not have you in this life.

I agree like a wrinkled feather falls from the tree
Light and white, you might still be all I see
In front of war, in midst of a cruel battle
My scars may burn from the sunshine
But I don't care to bleed if it makes you
Feel relieved that you could rely on me
You could count on me like a wrinkled feather ignored.

From the windows, outside on the grass
I notice in your arms where I longed to be scarred
One tear trickles down my burnt valleys
In my face, your face is carved on my sleeves.

Three flicks of fingers almost broken in the wind
And you won't remember me ever stepping here
But I'll remember like a curse I couldn't find a cure for
You'll linger in my town like an unrequited ghost.

The sword I used to fight for you
I'll be singing your ballet with it
Slithering across a cello, my sorrows in it
It should shriek but instead it cries
It cries in a melody you won't recognize.

'Heroes don't have happy endings'
Maybe you're not the love of my life
Just another lesson I spent my life
Figuring out in vain
Sweating my blood, burning my heart
Though I wish you were someone who saw me the same
But we're far apart from love, far apart from fame
I'm not the girl, at last you're not the king.

5. How stupid of me.

How stupid of me
To believe in black and blue
When white is all persists
And the world is hued.
My hands all coloured
I look up to the moon
It's all black and white
But then there's you.

How stupid of me
To run into you
Your face like fireworks
My town, all sad and doomed.
But you lit up the lamps
In each and every corner
Now I'm the light
You're my igniter.
But how stupid of me
To expect the town to burn
In flames of me and you

Wherein life, we learn
It's all messed up beneath.

How stupid of me
To call you 'my someone'
Whom I look up to when they say love
When they say I have something for someone.
How I wish it was me
Whom you'd sneak glances at
My whole year spent in your memories
And my ashes, flames burnt at.

How stupid of me
To stay up and until late night
For you to text or even a post
To hint something on our lore.
I thought I won when we sang
We won when you held my hand
But how little did I know that hand had held many
Like or not love, that hand had held many.

How stupid of me to
Think this is all about me
All about how the sky is beneath and my world above
My ground is nowhere but I'm here.
How I float in our oceans,
all filled with my tears

So sour, so blue,
It's almost three years.
Nothing could convince me
I'll stay for this long
Though I'm moving on,
Afraid this heart will hold on.

How too stupid of me
To think you had fallen for me too
You'd talk about messy things
and some kind of love undue.
My love all rented, never paid back
My skies all borrowed, never touched like that
How high you've gotten me, how low have I ever felt,
My love has morphed into a sweet goodbye.

How so stupid of me, I know, I know,
When love is so far and your light a glow
I've walked these woods for long,
And believe me, I loved every blind spot of it
But how stupid this love itself is
How stupid my love itself is
To delve in you had fallen for me too
To float in you had fallen for me too.

6. Home

Lights crept in, sneaking through the curtains
I looked outside to see it all so brightened
My eyes hurt, my legs sore, but I still make it out
Everyday I trampled on with no one to care about.

But one day I took a step through the door
I noticed your presence beside and I looked at your
Blue shirt and black hairs, taller than me if anyone cares
And my heart splattered my canvas into so many colours
Just your one glance made me suffer.

Bet you didn't notice me for long I know
November takes a long time to come too close
Your chapter in my life keeps going on like a song
Real old but still here like I've been here before.

The idea of you comes to me from time to time
Ascending the steps I feel closer in line
Sunsets shadow my fears and brighten my sight
I don't remember you, but you feel familiar all the time.

I read somewhere that it means you are the epitome
Of everything I've ever been subconsciously searching
home
Funny how universe works in ways they let us meet
I wouldn't want any other path to lead you to me.

Slowly I take steps and forget all around me
There's my dream, my likes and then you surrounding
My little world which will get bigger and bigger
I hope you'll stay with me through every other glitter.

Because there are no plans I foresee of you leaving my
path
I see you in my shadows I long to last
You were my home before you were familiar
I will go on to keep meeting you in every clear.

7. Parasite

Saying sorry was one way
And my endless talks the other
How long am I going to lie to you
Lie to myself the other.

Every time I step forward
Her thoughts take me back
Two steps at a time
But four steps back again
Again and again until her voice is
All that echoes in my mind
How she's so in love with you and
How I am not so kind.

My hands tempt me to touch you
Mould into something of mine
When I look in the mirror and see my scars
I wish you've the same with the similar lines
At one moment you are everything to me
Another, you're just another crime

I commit and bloody my hands
I smear them over my face
I look in the mirror and there I see
The person I am and someone I'm meant to be.

This love is alive, its breathing inside of me
Thinking of parting from you kills something in me
I feel like choking on thin air, my hands behind my back
Your face on the white walls and your voice in my head
This is mad and it feels forever for me
Its like a parasite, it's so free and unseen.

I've changed myself
I've changed my mind
I'm going to love you regardless
What's written in fate of mine
I told you we are meant to be
And I believe we've time
If we not so soon or near
I believe we've still time.

So I'll keep lying to you
I'll keep pretending to be someone I am not
Because I know I'm not benevolent, I'm not skinny
I'm not sure of my own insanity
But when it comes to you everything feels complete
Even if I am in pieces, you make every piece breathe

So with you I see the light and its burning warmth
Inside its core just a burning star
Just like my love for you, dying but bright
It'll disappear but we still have time.

8. For you to answer me

I walked up to the door
A rusty, rotten smell still lingering
I kept my stance and knocked upon the door
I waited in the darkness for you to answer me.

Sat down on the cold floor
Shivering, snowflakes falling down
Outside the window I see broken stars
They still shine and reach me
I wish upon the dying stars to teach me
How to live or die to be there
How to stay long in this space
For you to answer my prayer.

Crouched close to my scars
I can hear my beating heart
Its silent all around, I'm all I hear
How deafening is this silence
How awakening is my fear
A single sound I hear once

You wake me up by knocking twice.

I scurried up to the wood
I clutched it with my fingers
Pressing my face upon the bark
I tried to hear you whisper
I waited and held my breath
Your steps kept me awake
You circled the room and stopped again
You didn't knock again,
You didn't knock again.

I slept by the door
Frozen in the wind
Short of breath, short of some living
I haven't the seen the light in ages
I haven't seen it flickering
There's a constant sunset
And a lingering maze.

My eyes shut close,
Too devoid of energy to see you again
But when the wood thumped softly once
My eyes flew open and I winced a second at the dust
This time I knocked back
I called out your name
In the buried voices, I called out your name.

When I couldn't hear you back
I clutched it with my nails
I scratched upon the torn stencil
With a marred broken call
I'm withering, I'm crying, I'm dying in this
Without a second thought
I started banging on your door
I punched and ripped and clawed upon the rest
I screamed, I cried and it shrilled among the crest
I shouted, I shouted, I shouted for you to hear
One, two thuds and you were gone from fear.

I cried, I sank and I drowned in these voices
In this silence devoid of your presence
Windows now shattered, the sun is not shining
My eyes blind and I'm finally sleepy
I'm dreaming and trying to remember what it was
When willow and crawling ivy knocked upon my door
With flows and green and mosses grew upon the knob
I'm finally dreaming a dream of my own.

For you to answer me
I waited upon your shore
For you to answer me
I stood behind the door
For you to answer me

23

I looked out the window
For you to answer me
I felt no anger
I felt no anger.

9. Closure in blizzard

"You must be Eirlys, right?
I'm Ben, nice to meet you."
I would look up at your eyes
They'll remind me I've been here too.

The place seems familiar
Under your sky
You don't remember me
But I remember your goodbye.

Maybe this is the last time
We get to meet like this
But why am I the only one
Holding our memories.

Guess it was a storm trapped in silence
My feet got lost in the forest
A rustle from there, a sting right here
I kept walking until I found the crest.
You'll sit at your bench, unaware of it all

My hands will know, my heart will fear.

In italics I write your name in my book
You won't notice until you borrow it
'Can you say my name?' I could've asked you
But you didn't look my way, you went away.

You wave at me, to get my attention
You ask me if I play in the band
I'll nod and notice the same catchlights
Dancing but I know the steps this time.

I'll smile at you and tilt my head
Mock you for not knowing it
I'll tell you this and share some secrets
You'll be glad for me, my presence.

I'll make Jade jealous for choosing the wrong guy
She's so dumb, she can't see, our fate is intertwined
I know I love you, I know my heart lies to me
I know this will end, this time I won't let you be.

The day comes where I confess it to you
I held back this time and said it was someone else
You laughed and said you could convince them in a flick
I laughed and said if it was so easy, why wasn't it
already real?

You'll stare me in the eye and tilt your head
Mock me in my face and tell me secrets
We'll be good friends for long, my heart caged
When the day comes to say goodbye, I'll wave.

You won't look back, you don't care
You'll choose yourself over and over again
Jade may not be by your said, you were alone
I thought you wouldn't look back
I thought you wouldn't care.

But in came a ring on my doorstep
Ten years after, I see your face
I smile because my heart knows
I've lived it twice, my heart knows.

But you step forward and I don't move
You take my hand and whisper a secret
I know your name, know your lies
I don't know myself but I've lived you twice.

You'll hold my hand a little longer
The snow falling behind a little stronger
Some chill in the air but a mist between our breath
I've ruined it all but at least you're here.

A big part of my life, a chapter I've long closed
Who could be so dumb to keep going on and on
Walking alone, in storms, in rain, in a blizzard
All alone, shivering like a fool.

But you're here, and you've been here before
I see your foot marks and your habitual walk
You'll gaze in my eyes, not for long
You'll leave me alone but a note in my arms.

Crinkled as I opened, a snowflake marking the start
You said "It's over, a new start"
I look back at you and you're gone
What does it mean, what do you want?

You'll never answer, I'll never know
But we'll both nod in unison before
A long loved memory, a brushed open core
A heart pierced through me
But you held the notes.

10. Longing

In the midst of forgotten faces
For longer I remember your name
Sweeter your sound in my ears.

I'll wait till you come around
Smell your lavender
I know you'll come, I know you will
Just a trick of time,
I know we'll be fine.

When the sky turns grey
Our memories still stay
You're like the constellations
Bright perks swaying on my way
I look up at the sky
And breathe a little slower
Your beauty catches my soul
Your eyes all a little closer
Like the stars I can't touch
But the night like a cover.

Don't stop talking
Your voice is like a feeling
I'd die to feel
For the first time again.

Until we meet under the stars
At some concert or stage
Again, under the lights
You'll shine brighter.

This longing not so ancient
The fire still burns
Like its new, fiercer and prettier.
You smile like me and I sing like you
Inspire me everyday and I live for you
We live under the sun, in different timelines
But we met and that's all to say
This longing not so ancient
But all love in a different way.

11. Rodeo film

You play it like a photo reel, don't you?
Did you ever see me yearning for your eyes on me?
Should I say we were meant to dance on this floor
together,
And not you by her side in this movie?

Do you only notice my laugh?
Not the sweet misery under it's tones?
Not the casual flirt trying to reach your ears?
Not the smile I wear only for you?

Should we switch places?
How about you sit one afternoon
Staring out the window, into the clouds
Looking for the stars, making patterns
If ever into our connection.
Or let's sink in the pool one time
Let the water wash all our crimes
Come up to the surface, grasping for life
Only to realise how better it could've been by my side.

Play it like a rodeo film babe, watch all the scenes once
again,
Where I walk behind you not noticing my muffled steps
Where I sneak a look at you and draw you as my
princely mess
In this castle we walk in, this chatter of the school crowd
Everyone's a pawn in the game, we're the only crowns.

But then a twisting curve comes to the story
Your eyes fall on a maiden and she becomes your glory
The film glitches when it catches you staring at her
Because the film's mine, this stage is mine and not hers.

You see it crack and burn to flames
I watch you panicking in real and under an
overwhelming feeling
You try to correct it one time, you try to glance at the
remains, the other
I sit on my chair, waiting for it to be all over.

When we get out of the theatre, you call someone like
you missed her
I am walking by your side but you're not here with me
I hear her casual laugh and see your smile beaming in
glee.

What happened to our film reel, you ask?
Well it got burnt down to flames, if not last
I tore out the rest and scratched the left pieces
If this is all about her, if there's no you and me at last
I don't want to watch it like a rodeo film
I had hoped would be ours.

12. Brownish eyes

But between life and death,
Are those brownish eyes
My heart grasps onto my veins when you're around.
Your smell is like
Lavenders on my grave
I would want to unalive myself to breathe that again.

Your black hairs and
The curves around your neck.
Your red shirt pierces my soul with a haunting
attraction.
I'm drawn to you
Like a parallel line to it's same
You'll be my salvation in this mourning world I know.

You can call me yours and I would forget
How my name would feel like.
Our name on the clouds and my name on your lips
Your eyes say a million things,
A million words in a single stare

I am drawn to your aura as if I am being painted by
myself.

You're here beside me, and there's nothing I would want
more
Your smile lights up my darkest nights and blooms every
lily in my paradise
I should work hard and earn the reality to meet you
someday
We'll be good together, we can stay here forever.

When I saw your honey brown garden
My dreams started screaming your name
You're my one and only, you're my love
My yellow, my dreams, my everything in between.

So between life and death
Lie those brownish eyes for me
My love on the edge always
But your universe is carrying me
I am forever sailing in this sea
Of you and me.

13. Turning

Every time I look into your eyes
I feel things heavier than emotions
Like if skies could sing
They'll be singing a song of you to me
At the moment.

It's strange I've left behind the feeling
Of being forever with you, your voice
It's strange how I've grown over that obsession
But failing into this moment
Is like falling for a different version of you
All over again
I am repeating the same fairy-tale.

How can someone ever guess
The love I have for you in my eyes
How can you know
When I never show and tell
When I never wither to your side or crib at your
presence

When I don't talk to my friends about you.
You are the most beautiful thing for me in this world
I have to tell the flowers there is someone prettier than
them
Of course birds would be jealous
Someone sings better than them.

My diaries will know someone has taken over my heart
again
I am such a fragile thing, so vulnerable for attention
You are right here and right where I need you.
But you're there too.

Sometimes beside her, sometimes behind her,
I hate her, now or always did, I cannot know
But I know for sure what I don't like about you and her.
You're a terrible person for making me feel that way
Your fingers so beautiful, they're made for ne
Why run it for her? Why think about her,
when I am right here?

And just like that, it all comes down to jealousy, distress
and grief
What I have for you is turning into something ugly
Please stop this, come to me and say you like me too
Please say you'll want me over everything
Anew, aloof, as good as the moon,

Please.
Stop this nightmare and come to me.
I don't want you to leave.
I don't want me to leave.

14. Stephen

Stephen I don't know if you feel the same,
I try so hard to be the one I really am,
But I am afraid to show the parts of me,
No one knew were really mine.

Stephen I know there's no time like this in life,
We have got so much to do and little to feel about,
But I know you feel things, you feel things I don't know,
And I hope there's something of me you think about.

Stephen I know I should have told you,
I should have opened up my heart and said I have so
much more,
But I didn't, I was afraid to pluck any string of your
blood,
Which could tell you that I am not the one you could be
looking for.

Stephen I feel so happy when I am around you,
I feel the butterflies and moths, all tangled in a moon,

The shine I see in your eyes and the way you say the
words,
It all feels like a river of music flowing through my
bones.

Stephen I know I shouldn't have waved at you that day,
You were walking away but the thing was it that you
were looking my way,
My fingers go stiff and they want to make you smile,
So I waved and waved and waved till I knew it wasn't
fine.

Stephen I think I am drowning in this sea of your
paradise,
This poison is poisoning my wretched mind,
This feeling of everything to be just fit in the line.
It isn't making any sense to me than your smile.

Stephen I feel so overthinking my every word,
I wish you could clear what you always mean,
I don't seem to get it ever, ever and ever,
I don't think I'll be okay till the next September.

Stephen I know we can't be together,
This time, this stream, this call for everything,
Doesn't sit in a room of our responsibilities,
This isn't right, I know.

Stephen I wish you were the reason I don't believe in
love,
But you are making it seem simple and real,
These unspoken words of yours and your sweet, sweet
smile,
Its making my heart jump a million times into the
pitfalls of me.

15. Stardust

Were you made of stardust?
Your eyes spoke so many languages in glitters for me,
Decorating my sky with tiny dots of memories,
I wonder if I would've gone blind from the light.

Want to go over the moon?
Your voice flowing like a melody through my nerves,
Making me vulnerable day by day to your presence,
You're an art and I am just a small curve under your
name.

Is happiness always with us?
Its for eternity with you, in your smile and the coffee
you brew,
From waking up in the morning to working 12 hours a
day,
I am up to see your face one day.

12 ages later, were you jealous?
Seeing me walking with someone else besides the road,

Turning your wheel towards us, your heart burns for the
love
It aches for it was empty all along, you brought the heat
back but after how long?

The fur was black, did you hold it close enough?
Can I reach out from your grasp and hold the soul near,
Mould it into a thing of mine and make it clear
That you were made for me and not someone other
I am here and you should be near.

The moon is pretty, isn't it?
Could I hear those words from your dried lips,
Kiss and tell the ones watching us,
You blend into me so perfectly like salt in sugar
You twist in my ways and I breathe the clear.

So tell me were you made of stardust?
Cause my hands now reflect spots from the cuts
Bruised from the times you couldn't make it clear
Back to the moon, our love lost in the lights,
I am not blind yet and you're not in my sight, so
If you were stardust, I should be the starlight.

But there's no you, no dust in the sky
My world's now a desert under the night
It's cold and I'm shivering in the folds

43

You and I were close,
but you were not the stardust I was looking for.

16. Moon

Never mind how many hands I cross
You can say I can't touch yours
We feel present and we stare for long
How many seconds passed since you saw that in me?

Past your sight once a day I walk
Accidentally or fortuitously, you were all I saw
The world stood silent when you smiled at me
Not red or blue, but all white and always unseen.

There's something I miss
Something I can't notice about you
You're the kind of haven I've long chased for
But I can't decipher this all through.

Every time we talk and look at each other
Your sympathetic eyes erase all my colours
All the paints merging into one single hue
The colour of it is blind to my moon.

How can someone become such an irony like me
Caring in the head and indifferent in between
My texts lay haunted on your desk
You pick them up like pieces of chess.

This similarity I feel inside my head
We look for fun, we chase after breath
I forget to sleep, you sleep to rest
Still in between with same shoes ahead.

You were the first, you'll always be the last
There'll be many on the path as I'm far too gone to part
I live for that mess, I live for that noon
You walk past me, and I walk on to you.

Your drinks in front of me and my heart open to you,
I won't take yours, you won't take me any soon,
Because I know I am a wanderer and you're so unfused,
We're both detached from what should be true.

Still I'll sit in the cafes, at night looking for you
I know you'll come and I'll wave at you
Your blue cap and my glassy eyes,
What a combination of pretty lies.

17. Circles

I'm not feeling well again tonight
Your thoughts creep up to me like spiders in sight
It's the thing I fear the most, your rejection like ice
No matter how many songs about you I write
I can never shake off this feeling I get from you.

It's like I'm dragging my feet now out of the mud
Out of the ditch I've made up of myself and fallen into
There's no one around, no one to help me out
You were never here in this place I've started calling
home
The place I built from the mess you made of me
Tearing me into parts I never imagined of me.

I wish you'd hit me up with those internet jokes you
found
You'll sit back and laugh, and I'll just watch you to sore
To the point where I don't know where I am or who am I
To the depths where exist only you and I
Because you're the only haven I've ever known

Love at first sight maybe so, you're the only haven I've
ever known.

Withdrawal symptoms are catching up to me now that
you're gone
I can't look at the skies without thinking of you anymore
The sights of stars and moon almost tear me up every
night
How you used to say if I watched it or not
If I missed some eclipse or some godly sort at a random
time
I really miss you if anything else
I really miss you if it means anything to you.

I don't know what I'm waiting for this late at night
I don't know what is this feeling I just can't shake off
The moment I saw you I knew my heart will remember
this for long
Why so pretty, why so tall, why so much like the person
I want
To heal my scars and heal my sins
As if I can be pure if I have been sinned
You'll make it all disappear I believe
You'll make it all disappear like the wind you're in.

You don't deserve to hurt me like this but here you are
Tripping on parts of me I've long scarred

Breaking all the waves and hollowing my heart
You're an addiction I just can't get cleared.

I rewind every moment I can of you
Why is love never reciprocated the way I want it to
You keep me going in circles I can't seem to break
You keep calling me back when I said I won't stay
Because these red strings tangled in me are now choking
me to death
You're the only person I've known who can kill me just
like that
Without a single word, without another glance
Without a doubt of who I am.

18. Imagine

Because something as dangerous as love
It's better to be destroyed by it
Than to live with it.

But you make it feel so easy
You make it feel like pieces of me are just pebbles in the
sea
Step by step we cross the whole ocean
Barefaced and borrowed, we measure our emotions
You smile at me and I forget all locations
Just your heart dotting to mine
Your hands intertwined with mine.

I used to wake up breathless and soured
From nightmares of life and happiness never savoured
Regrets float across my eyes, a single tear drop this time
But now I wake up with your hands there to erase it
My marks all gone being lost in your mazes
Too busy to look at the sky now, you're my whole
universe

Cold winds blow through the curtains and I'm dreaming
in your covers.

Life, so beautiful to forget what pain felt like
Your laugh locked in me like a sun to its flower
Shining bright, I'm so happy to have you beside me
I cannot explain the ways in which you bind me
To hope, to dreams, to happiness that we share
Your voice is a healer in itself
No need to dare.

You make my thoughts run like butterflies in a field
Free and beyond any boundaries
How can something be so ironic and forgiving at the
same time
So pretty and dangerous in the same line
Guess it depends on who holds the pen
To write our story, I hope its in your hands.

Because I'm such a wreck, I cannot even imagine being
in love
I like it messy, ruined to the core, it satisfies my soul
But you step in and everything goes silent
No heartbeats, no breath, just your eyes and,
I forget how wrong I am and how wronged I've been
Sins I committed and broken glasses no more to be seen
Just that pen and your sight beside me

I'm so lucky to have you
I'm so grateful to be seen.

19. Line

In the midst of broken promises
I hear them swirling through the lips to my ears
My trembling fingers cover my ears in a calm fright
What am I afraid of I don't even know
When I no longer have any promise to break
My wishes sailed from the shore and drowned in the
ocean somewhere
Your skin softened in that ocean of my tears
You're no longer here so what are these promises made
of?
This broken heart still scared of?

Every step I take through our valley of life
That chapter where you walked beside me all the time
My shoulders now falter from the weight of your eyes on
me
That memory still clear in my head, still serene
But that peace is marred with colours I no longer
recognize
Your face is blur to me in this valley of time

Then who am I afraid of in this chapter of lies?
When you're no longer here, what is it that still lingers,
Beyond my comprehension,
Beyond our own time.

When I pick those cups your hands once had touched,
This haunted house still reminds me of you so much
How come a place I built first
Becomes something I can no longer breathe in
Somewhere you just walked out of
And it felt like the whole air was sucked out
Just as you scratched my heart till it's last caress
You took my everything with you including my shed
I walk in boots, I no longer care
Then why does this thought lingers that you robbed me
of my share?
That you robbed me of everything I could ever bear.

Just as the rivers flow on and on
I thought some things do last beyond
The bars that were once created
The premonitions which were never debated
I thought you'd be the one who'd walk over that bar with
me
Hand in hand, in our eyes no guilt
Of course you're mine and I'm yours
Then how did those bars cut over me?

I shielded you from the storm but you never thought of
me
You disappeared in wind, then why did you follow me?
Those broken promises with prays of love
How can you be so clever but never enough for us?

Seems like there's only one answer to this
No lies, no promise, no me
This love that still breathes in these things which you left
behind
Promises which you could never bind
And the house that still stands still in time
Love breaks apart but reality is all the lie
Before me stands a bar and I still have time
But that strength is so forgotten I don't even remember it
being mine
Just your touch which once held mine
I never stopped loving you
I could never stop loving you
Even if you're not here
Even if this silence is all I hear
Line after line like a siren
Life is so unforgiven.

20. Kill

Everyone told me to get separated from you,
But look at my broken heart,
it's so stubborn for you.

The moment you got insecure about your looks
Your colour and your tanned tunes,
Your curls were all binding me to you in the dark,
I had zero intention to call you out in front of everyone,
But that's just who I am when it comes to you.

So loud and unapologetic, I don't know where my
uncaged self will take me,
Though I hope it takes me into the arms of someone like
you,
Someone like you, if not you,
Because I am so lonely, I could eat my fingers away
when I am alone,
Uncaged self and so unknown,
To myself, I am so alone.

That time when they told me to sing a song from three
words,
I could only think of how I could sneak you in my world,
And make it all yours, that time, that night,
Just to make it all yours.

You don't even notice me when I am around, and
honestly I don't even care,
But sometimes when I sit with myself, your voice is all I
hear,
You didn't walk along to drop me off, but you did to bade
someone else,
What more proof do I need to clear it once and for all,
Just like that song I heard before my eyes met yours,
We were meant to be not made to last at all.

Delusion is such a crazy thing for once,
I remember being in places with you we never crossed,
How sickening if someone else reads my mind,
How rotten it is by my own crimes,
Dead memories of you I still touch to keep alive,
Never breathing your scent, just carbon dioxide.

I know I will go on, that's what I do when I remember
you're not a friend of mine,
Because friends remember each other at times,
They touch and keep things alive,

Buried or burnt, or just ghosted to survive,
You never reached me to ever call yourself at least a
friend of mine.

Though you're not even a friend, not even someone I
could have something about to remember on,
We just happened to meet and I got lost in your eyes,
that's all,
Lost in your eyes, that's all,
I've always been decisive and a companion of myself for
years,
But just one look of yours and I forget who I am,
All that flower I garlanded for me,
And I forget who I am.

21. You can't die

You sneaked up to me when I searched how to die
I was afraid you'd find out, I was afraid to lie
Your eyes seemed full of life and your smile so bright
The sun reflected your happiness but shadowed mine.

I can't say I never wanted to say goodbye
I've either been on tip toes or crawled my way to life
It's so unforgiving-how can I survive
On few drops given and an ocean all dried.

I really want to give up, I still want to die
Damn there's no way better out of this sight
A crumpling body or a dying smile
Never knew death came in so many faces like lies.

You came to me and I said a weakened 'Hi'
I packed my bags and left the room as before
We played games and you talked to me normally
We both knew what was going on and what was
supposed to be truly.

I met you while you were cycling on the pass beside
So bright and happy just like the yellow sunshine
I know fate is unforgiving but at least it shares
Some parts of me to you and yours to mine.

Some can never say out loud, some can never try
Your all black shirt and my past tries
You evade your eyes from my sight
And that's all the hint I need more to not try.

But I still walk all over my mistakes
I don't look back, I don't think twice
If life is such stubborn, I was born heartless
We grow up, we shed our skins,
that's all the reason we need to say goodbye.